Diet recommendations during TCM - Stomach - Food Stagnation

Please check these recommendations always with a nutrition consultant, therapist, doctor or dietician. The recipes and the list of ingredients are supporting the conventional medical therapy. The calorie disclosures of fresh ingredients (fruit and vegetables) vary according to quality and time of harvest. The contents were checked by a dietician and a nutrition consultant for the Traditional Chinese Medicine (TCM).

Author:
©2020 Josef Miligui
www.ebns.at

Source:
The lists are created from the EBNS database for nutritional counseling. The database is used by dietitians, therapists and doctors for advising the patient / client.

Literature:
The specialist literature and the training documents of the German and Austrian dietary and traditional Chinese medicine serve as a knowledge base. We have used the documents as a basis of knowledge, adapted it to our experience and completed them.
http://nutribook.info/

Production and publishing:
BoD – Books on Demand, Norderstedt
ISBN: 9783752893977

Diet recommendations for TCM - Stomach - Food stagnation

1   Treatment strategy

Eliminate stagnation, direct stomach QI down.
Hot NO, warm neutral YES (except sour), refreshing LITTLE, cold NO

2   Avoid

Large meals with many ingredients, too much food, eat late,
indigestible, too much meat and cereals
(bread), sour taste, spicy, breaded, fried, grilled, too dry food, cheese-
baked, dairy products.

3   Breakfast   kkal. per serving

Apple sauce with raisins	73
Barley soup	265
Barley water	44
Radish with horseradish	196
Rice congee with carrots and fennel	131
Rice noodle soup with shiitake mushrooms	65
Rice porridge with orange peel	119
Tea from savory	1
Tea from thyme	0
Tea Green tea	2
Tsampa	139

4 Snack

5 Lunch

6 Afternoon

7 Dinner

8 Any time

9 Recipes

(rec.) = You can use more.
(little) = You should use less than specified
(omit) = omit.

9.1 8 treasures of rice

Strengthens kidney and bladder, builds up Qi, strengthens the spleen, repels moisture, reduces internal heat, prevents cancer, builds heart, calms nerves.
Cooking time approx. 1 hour
Calories p. portion: 212
4 portions

Quantity of ingredients
Lily bulbs 1 table spoon / 5g. () - cool - sweet, bitter .... *
Longane 1 table spoon / 5g. (yes) - warm - sweet .... *
King Solomon's-seal 1 table spoon / 5g. () - neutral - sweet, bitter .... *
Yam root, yam root tuber 1 table spoon / 5g. () - neutral - sweet .... *
Coix (seeds) YiYi Ren 1 table spoon / 5g. (little) - cool - sweet, neutral .... *
Rice wild (nature rice) 1 1/2 cups / 240g. (yes) - neutral - sweet, bitter..... metal
Water 8-10 cups / 800g. (yes) - cool - salty..earth

Cooking instructions:
Each one 1 tbsp: Bai He, Longan, Yu Zhu, Da Zao, Shan Yao, Lian Mi, Yi Yi Ren, Qian Shi Add hot water and soak for about 30 minutes. Then add 1 - 2 cups of rice (normal) and simmer for 1/2 to 1 hour until the rice is very soft. Or: Cook for about 3 hours with the herbs a congee. Then the herbs do not have to be soaked.

9.2 Apple sauce with raisins

Nourishes fluids, reduces stomach heat, strengthens spleen, harmonizes stomach, moisturizes, relaxes, builds up Qi.
Cooking time approx. 25 min
Calories p. portion: 74
10 portions
Allergens: O

Quantity of ingredients
Apple (sweet) 2,2 lbs / 1000g. (rec.) - cool - sweet, sour ....earth
Water 1/2 cup / 100g. (yes) - cool - salty...earth
Raisins 1/8 lbs - 2oz / 50g. (yes) - warm - sweet.......................................earth

Cooking instructions:
Wash, peel and quarter the apples and remove the core. Put the apples with the water in a pot. Wash the raisins with hot water and add them. Cook at low heat for about 10 minutes, then allow to cool. For children up to 10 months, mash in the blender finely. For the larger ones, crush with the potato steamer. Fill and seal in a freezer or empty yoghurt jug. Close the yoghurt jug. Freeze in the shock freezer.
If necessary, thaw at room temperature for about 6 hours. (Lasting about 4 months).
The fruit mousse is intended as dessert or intermediate meal. It has an anti-digestive effect. In case of diarrhea give better banana.

9.3   Barley soup

Works neutral to slightly warming and relaxes the Qi flow. Helps with loss of appetite and diarrhea due to spleen weakness. With weak spleen qi, one should often eat salty soups for breakfast.
Cooking time approx. 25 min
Calories p. portion: 265
2 portions
Allergens: A

Quantity of ingredients
Barley 1 cup / 120g. (rec.) - cool - sweet, little salty ....earth
Salt 1 pinch / 1g. (yes) - cold - salty ....water
Ginger fresh 1/2 teaspoon / 1g. (rec.) - warm - acrid................................metal
Olive oil 1 table spoon / 10g. (little) - cool - sweet.....................................earth
Parsley 3 table spoons / 30g. (rec.) - warm - bitter....................................wood
Water 1 1/2 cups / 240g. (yes) - cool - salty...earth

Cooking instructions:
Roast the barley in the pan, then grind it to the ground, and boil with water, some salt and ginger to a mash. Before serving add oil and parsley.

Variant: You can add a better taste to the dish if you cook it with prepared vegetable or meat broth.

9.4 Barley water

Moisturizes the lungs and large intestine, forces spleen, cools bladder, moisturizes intestines, relaxes, builds up
 Qi, spreads, forces spleen, passes downwardly.
Cooking time approx. 2 hours
Calories p. portion: 44
10 portions
Allergens: A

Quantity of ingredients
Barley 1/4 lbs - 4oz / 100g. (rec.) - cool - sweet, little salty ....earth
Water 8 cup - 1/2 1 Gallon / 1900g. (yes) - cool - salty ....earth
Lemon peel 1 knife tip / 1g. (little) - cool - bitter...fire
Cinnamon ground 1 pinch / 1g. () - hot - acrid, sweet .... *
Fig 4-5 pieces / 100g. (yes) - warm - sweet ....earth
Ginger fresh 1 pinch / 1g. (rec.) - warm - acrid...metal
Clove 1 piece / 0,5g. (yes) - warm - acrid...metal
Salt 1 pinch / 1g. (yes) - cold - salty ....water
Cocoa 1 pinch / 1g. () - warm - sweet, bitter..fire

Cooking instructions:
Give the barley in a pot of 2 l. water and let it swell for 5 hours. Then heat the barley, add the fig, cinnamon, clove, ginger and salt. Simmer for 2 hours and strain the hot barley water. Add the grated lemon peel and cocoa.

9.5 Basic recipe for a chicken broth worming

Strengthens Qi and blood, is very warm.
Cooking time approx. 2-3 hours
Calories p. portion: 90
9 portions
Allergens: L

Quantity of ingredients
Chicken meat 1/2 piece / 600g. (little) - warm - sweet............................... wood
Carrot 2 pieces / 150g. (rec.) - neutral - sweet...earth
Leek 1 stick / 45g. (yes) - warm - acrid ....metal
Celery root 1 piece / 500g. (yes) - cool - sweet..earth
Ginger fresh 2 slices / 2g. (rec.) - warm - acrid ....metal
Juniper berry 1 teaspoon / 3g. (yes) - warm - sweet, acrid, bitter.................fire
Bay leaf 3 pieces / 2g. () - warm - acrid.. *
Water 4 cup / 900g. (yes) - cool - salty..earth

Cooking instructions:

Remove chicken parts from fat. Place chicken pieces in a saucepan with hot water and heat till it boils briefly, skimming any resulting foam. Add coarsely chopped vegetables and all spices and cook over medium heat for 2 to 3 hours. Strain the finished soup. Throw away vegetables and bones.

Tip: If you want to use the meat as a soup insert, take out after 45 minutes and return only the bones in the soup.

Refrigerate for later use.

9.6 Basic recipe for a duck broth

Forces Qi, strengthens blood and fluids, nourishes Yin, forces stomach, cools heat, strengthens spleen and liver.
Cooking time approx. 2-3 hours
Calories p. portion: 61
6 portions
Allergens: L

Quantity of ingredients

Water 2 cup / 450g. (yes) - cool - salty..earth
Duck (heart) 5/8 oz / 200g. (little) - cool - sweet.......................................wood
Duck (slaughtered) 1/4 lbs - 4oz / 100g. (little) - cool - sweet, salty ....wood
Carrot 2 pieces / 100g. (rec.) - neutral - sweet...earth
Celery root 1/2 piece / 600g. (yes) - cool - sweet.......................................earth

Cooking instructions:

Cook duck pieces with vegetables for 2-3 hours. Sift broth through a fine sieve and refrigerate for later use.

The innards can be reused: You cut them finely and leaves them for a few minutes with fresh vegetables in the broth draw. Sprinkle with parsley before serving.

9.7 Basic recipe for a reissue soup (Congee)

Warms the stomach and spleen, harmonizes the intestine, forces Qi, reduces moisture.
Cooking time approx. 2-4 hours
Calories p. portion: 140
3 portions

Quantity of ingredients
Rice variety any 1 cup / 120g. (yes) - warm - sweet.................................. metal
Water 6 cups / 700g. (yes) - cool - salty ....earth

Cooking instructions:
Cook rice and water in a ratio of about 1: 6. The amount of water determines the thickness of the mash (matter of taste).
Put the rice in a saucepan with a heavy lid. It is important to simmer the rice after a short boil on the slightest flame, otherwise it burns.
Boil the rice for 2-4 hours. The longer he cooks, the more he strengthens.
If you want to eat the dish for breakfast, you can put the rice on just before bedtime.
To be on the safe side, you should first check the behavior of your pot and cooker under observation for a similar amount of time, so that nothing burns.
Refrigerate for later use.

9.8   Celery juice

Strengthens stomach Qi, moisturizes, relaxes, builds up Qi, spreads.
Cooking time approx. 5 min
Calories p. portion: 33
1 portions
Allergens: L

Quantity of ingredients
Celery root 1/2 piece / 200g. (yes) - cool - sweet ....earth
Water 1 cup / 120g. (yes) - cool - salty...earth
Salt 1 pinch / 0,5g. (yes) - cold - salty ....water

Cooking instructions:
Peel celeriac and cut into pieces and juice. Mix with water and salt as needed.

9.9   Chicken soup with egg yolk and parsley

Forces Qi and blood, is very warming, nourishes blood and liver, harmonizes liver and spleen, forces eyesight, preserves the fluids, contracts.
Cooking time approx. 10 min
Calories p. portion: 118
2 portions
Allergens: CL

Quantity of ingredients
Basic recipe for a chicken soup (warming) 2 cup / 500g. (yes) - warm - *........ *
Chicken yolk 1 piece / 10g. (little) - neutral - sweet ....earth
Parsley 1 table spoon / 10g. (rec.) - warm - bitter .... wood

Cooking instructions:
Cook the chicken broth according to the basic recipe.
Heat broth and bubble the egg yolk. Sprinkle the chopped parsley over it and let it rest for about 2 minutes. Drink in small sips.

9.10 Clear soup from goose

Forces spleen, stomach and lungs, relieves weakness, forces Qi, calms the stomach, gets Qi moving, directs upwards, strengthens spleen and liver, regulates Qi flow, moisturizes, relaxes, builds up Qi, spreads.
Cooking time approx. 2-3 hours
Calories p. portion: 334
6 portions

Quantity of ingredients
Goose parts 1,1 lbs / 500g. (little) - neutral - sweet................................... metal
Carrot 1 piece / 100g. (rec.) - neutral - sweet...earth
Onion (shallot) 1 piece / 25g. (yes) - warm - acrid, sweet .... metal
Leek 1 piece / 250g. (yes) - warm - acrid .... metal
Parsley 1 Twig / 4g. (rec.) - warm - bitter .... wood
Lovage 1 Twig / 4g. (yes) - warm - acrid, bitter .... metal
Lovage 1 Twig / 4g. (yes) - warm - acrid, bitter .... metal
Water 4 cup / 1000g. (yes) - cool - salty...earth
Salt 1 pinch / 0,5g. (yes) - cold - salty .... water

Cooking instructions:
Simmer goose pieces with vegetables and herbs for 2-3 hours. Sift through a fine cloth and cool. Degrease and store in the refrigerator.

9.11 Grapefruit juice

Nourishes fluids, passes downwardly, forms body fluid.
Cooking time approx. 5 min
Calories p. portion: 107
1 portions

Quantity of ingredients

Grapefruit (Pomelo) 1 cup / 250g. (rec.) - cool - sweet, sour.........................fire

Cooking instructions:
Juice fresh grapefruit or use organic juice.

9.12 Japanese algae soup

Strengthens spleen and liver, regulates Qi flow, moisturizes, relaxes, builds up Qi, spreads, nourishes the lungs and spleen, distributes mucus, dissolves mucus, dissolves stagnation, directs upwards, gets Qi moving und Yang.
Cooking time approx. 20 min
Calories p. portion: 47
3 portions

Quantity of ingredients

Wakame 1 oz / 25g. (little) - cold - salty ....water
Water 2 cup / 450g. (yes) - cool - salty...earth
Onion (shallot) 1-2 pcs. / 30g. (yes) - warm - acrid, sweet ....metal
Radish (white, green, purple-red) 1/8 lbs - 2oz / 50g. (rec.) - cool - sweet, acrid
  metal
Carrot 2 pieces / 180g. (rec.) - neutral - sweet..earth
Miso 2 table spoons / 20g. (rec.) - neutral - salty ....water
Parsley 2 table spoons / 20g. (rec.) - warm - bitter....................................wood
Onion (spring onion) 1 table spoon (sliced)...metal

Cooking instructions:
Soak wakame in water for a few minutes, remove and bring the water to the boil. Add finely chopped onions and wakame, radishes and carrots, cut into thin strips, and simmer for another 10 minutes. Dissolve miso in a little cooled cooking water and add it at the end. Sprinkle with parsley and spring onions.

9.13 Pumpkin soup

Forces lungs and spleen, diuretic, forces Qi, protects liver, forces Qi, forces spleen, relieves inflammation, moisturizes, relaxes, builds up Qi, spreads, strengthens spleen and liver, regulates Qi flow, moisturizes, relaxes, builds up Qi, spreads.
Cooking time approx. 1 hour
Calories p. portion: 105
3 portions

Quantity of ingredients

Pumpkin 3/4 lbs / 300g. (yes) - warm - sweet ....earth
Carrot 2 pieces / 100g. (rec.) - neutral - sweet..earth
Potato 2 pieces / 120g. (yes) - neutral - sweet...earth
Olive oil 1 table spoon / 10g. (little) - cool - sweet......................................earth
Onion white 1 piece / 50g. (yes) - warm - acrid...metal
Water 1 cup / 120g. (yes) - cool - salty...earth
Parsley 1 table spoon / 7g. (rec.) - warm - bitter ....wood
Anise (Common Fennel) 1 pinch / 1g. (yes) - warm - acrid ....earth
Salt 1 pinch / 1g. (yes) - cold - salty ....water

Cooking instructions:

Add the olive oil to the pan, add the diced pumpkin, diced carrots and potatoes. Roast them shortly, add the finely chopped onion, fill with water, add enough water to cover the vegetables at least 3 finger-widths. Boil at low heat.

Season with sea salt, add small cutted parsley, a pinch of anise (little). Allow to simmer for about 35 minutes. Then purée the soup and add some water, depending on the consistency of
the soup.

9.14 Radish with horseradish

Slightly refreshing and moisturizing, dissolves stagnation, nourishes blood and liver, harmonizes liver and spleen, forces eyesight, preserves the fluids, contracts, nourishes the lungs and spleen, distributes mucus, dissolves mucus, dissolves stagnation,
Cooking time approx. 30 min
Calories p. portion: 196
2 portions
Allergens: GNO

Quantity of ingredients

Butter organic 1 table spoon / 8g. (yes) - neutral - sweet...........................earth
Radish (white, green,) 1/2 piece / 50g. (rec.) - cool - sweet, acrid ....metal
Water 3 table spoons / 10g. (yes) - cool - salty ....earth
Lemon juice 2 table spoons / 20g. () - cold - sour ....wood
White wine 2 table spoons / 20g. (yes) - cool - sweet, bitter, acrid...........wood
Pepper powder (hot) 1 pinch / 0,2g. () - warm - bitter....................................fire
Sesame oil 1 teaspoon / 3g. (little) - cool - sweet......................................earth
Radish horseradish 2 table spoons / 20g. () - neutral - sweet, little acrid ..metal
Salt 1 pinch / 0,5g. (yes) - cold - salty ....water
Parsley 1 Bunch (chopped) / 80g. (rec.) - warm - bitter..............................wood
Rice long grain rice 1/2 cup / 60g. (yes) - neutral - sweet ....metal

Water 3 cups / 300g. (yes) - cool - salty ....earth
Salt 1 pinch / 0,5g. (yes) - cold - salty ....water

Cooking instructions:
In a hot pan melt the butter, sautéed into stripes cut radish. Add cold water, lemon juice, white wine, a pinch of rose paprika and stir in the sesame oil; with 2 - 3 tablespoons fresh grated horseradish (alternatively 1 teaspoon from the glass), salt to taste; Sprinkle with chopped parsley.

Place the rice with the water, salt and cook for about 15 minutes.

9.15 Rice congee with carrots and fennel

Nutritious builds up Qi, forces the digestive functions.
Cooking time approx. 2 hours and more
Calories p. portion: 131
3 portions
Allergens: G

Quantity of ingredients
Basic recipe for a rice soup (Congee) 2 cup / 500g. (yes) - neutral - sweet ..... *
Carrot 2 pieces / 100g. (rec.) - neutral - sweet ....earth
Fennel 1 piece / 250g. (yes) - warm - sweet, little acrid ....earth
Butter organic 1 teaspoon / 3g. (yes) - neutral - sweet..............................earth
Cardamom 1/2 teaspoon / 1g. () - warm - acrid.. *

Cooking instructions:
Cook rice congee according to basic recipe.
Clean and cut carrots and fennel.

When carrots and fennel are cooked from the beginning, they serve wholesomeness. If added shortly before the end of the cooking time, taste and vitamins are retained.

Refine with butter and cardamom before serving.

9.16 Rice noodle soup with shiitake mushrooms

Strengthens spleen and liver, regulates Qi flow, relaxes, builds up Qi, spreads, dries out, passes downwardly, strengthens stomach Qi, nourishes Yin of the lungs, stomach and colon, supports digestion, reduces internal wind.
Cooking time approx. 20 min
Calories p. portion: 66
2 portions
Allergens: L

Quantity of ingredients
Rice noodles 2 handful / 20g. (yes) - neutral - sweet .... metal
Shiitake, dried 4-6 pieces / 5g. (yes) - neutral - sweet .... earth
Basic recipe for a vegetable soup (nutritious) 1 1/2 cups / 240g. () - neutral - **
Chinese cabbage 1 cup / 60g. (yes) - cool - sweet .... earth
Lovage 1 teaspoon / 3g. (yes) - warm - acrid, bitter .... metal
Miso 2 table spoons / 18g. (rec.) - neutral - salty .... water

Cooking instructions:
Soak rice noodles and shiitake mushrooms separately in cold water. Heat the vegetable broth and add the soaked shiitake mushrooms cut into strips and simmer gently. Cut Chinese cabbage into noodles, add lovage green and rice noodles and let it steep for a while. Before serving, stir in Miso dissolved in a little cooled water.
 Recommendation: Suitable at the beginning of each meal, also for breakfast

9.17 Rice porridge with orange peel

Warms the stomach and spleen, harmonizes the intestine, forces Qi, reduces moisture. brings the Liver Qi in motion, cools heat, moisturizes, relaxes, builds up Qi, spreads. nourishes blood, moisturizes, relaxes, builds up Qi, spreads.
Cooking time approx. 10 min
Calories p. portion: 120
4 portions
Allergens: L

Quantity of ingredients

Rice variety any 1 cup / 100g. (yes) - warm - sweet.................................. metal
Water 6 cups / 600g. (yes) - cool - salty..earth
Olive oil 1 table spoon / 10g. (little) - cool - sweet ....earth
Champignon 1/2 cup / 50g. (little) - cool - sweet ....earth
Celery sticks 1/2 bunch / 60g. (rec.) - cool - sweet.....................................earth
Basic recipe for a chicken soup 3-4 table spoons / 40g. (yes) - warm - *......... *
Salt 1 pinch / 0,5g. (yes) - cold - salty .... water

Cooking instructions:

The day before boil the rice with the orange peel and water in a ratio of about 1: 6. The amount of water determines the thickness of the mash (pure matter of taste). Put the rice in a saucepan with good insulation and a heavy lid. It is important to simmer the rice after a short boil on the slightest flame, otherwise it burns. Boil the rice for 2-4 hours. The longer he cooks, the more he strengthens.
Heat the oil in a saucepan, add the chopped champignon and celery and sauté briefly. Add the rice. Add vegetable broth or water, warm up, salt.

9.18 Spice liqueur

Warms the middle, passes downwardly, tonifies the kidney-Yang, warms kidneys and spleen, forces Qi.
Cooking time approx. 20 min
Calories p. portion: 19
10 portions

Quantity of ingredients

Cardamom 1 oz / 30g. () - warm - acrid.. *
Sugar candy white 2 table spoons / 20g. (yes) - neutral - sweet ....earth
Spirit 1 cup / 300g. () - hot - sour... metal

Cooking instructions:

Pour all the ingredients in a wide-mouthed bottle with the schnapps and leave in a dark place for at least 7 days (better still longer).

A glass after a fatty meal regulates stomach energy.

9.19 Spring vegetables

Cools heat, diuretic, cools blood, reduces mucus, moisturizes, relaxes, builds Qi, distributes, strengthen the middle, nourishes lung Yin, produces humors.
Cooking time approx. 1 1/2 hour
Calories p. portion: 64
8 portions
Allergens: G

Quantity of ingredients
Carrot 1,1 lbs / 500g. (rec.) - neutral - sweet..earth
Kohlrabi 1,1 lbs / 500g. (yes) - neutral - acrid, sweet ....earth
Butter organic 2 table spoons / 20g. (yes) - neutral - sweet ....earth
Water 1/2 cup / 125g. (yes) - cool - salty..earth

Cooking instructions:
Wash the vegetables thoroughly. Clean and peel carrots and turnip cabbage. From the turnip cabbage, finely chop some delicate leaves and set aside. Rasp the carrots and the turnip cabbage. Melt the butter, add the water and the vegetables and cook over medium heat for about 30 minutes. Stir occasionally. Spread the vegetables and cooked water to about 8 deep-frozen bags to a100-150 g (depending on the age of the child). Close the bags, allow them to cool down and freeze them for max 3 months.
If necessary, thaw, boil and mix with 80g of boiled potatoes and an egg. (The recipe can easily be varied if you want to use cauliflower, peas or zucchini)

9.20 Tea from celery sticks

Brings the Liver Qi in motion, cools heat, moisturizes, relaxes, builds up Qi, spreads.
Cooking time approx. 15 min
Calories p. portion: 1
4 portions
Allergens: L

Quantity of ingredients
Celery sticks 2 table spoons (chopped) / 18g. (rec.) - cool - sweet............earth
Water 2 cup / 500g. (yes) - cool - salty...earth

Cooking instructions:
Heat the water till it boils and put it aside. Add cutted celery and cook
for 10 min. to let go. Strain. Sweet to taste with honey.

9.21 Tea from ground

Reduces mucus and moist heat in the liver and gallbladder, against liver
Qi stagnation, spleen qi deficiency, spleen and kidney Yang-Mangel.
Cooking time approx. 10 min
Calories p. portion: 2
4 portions

Quantity of ingredients
Ground 1 teaspoon / 3g. (rec.) - warm - acrid .... metal
Water 2 cup / 500g. (yes) - cool - salty..earth

Cooking instructions:
Heat the water till it boils and put it aside. Add crushed cumin and leave
for 10 min. to let go. Sweet to taste with honey. Strain when pouring.

Drink 1 cup 2 times a day.

9.22 Tea from savory

Tonifies the kidney-Yang, the stomach and spleen Qi and warms the
middle, forces the liver Qi and the blood, conducts mucus and cold from
the lungs, opens the surface, derives wind-cold.
Cooking time approx. 10 min
Calories p. portion: 1
4 portions

Quantity of ingredients
Savory 2-4 teaspoons / 9g. (rec.) - warm - bitter .... water
Water 2 cup / 500g. (yes) - cool - salty..earth

Cooking instructions:
Brew dried savory with boiling water and cover for about 10 minutes.
Strain the tea and drink warm.

9.23 Tea from thyme

Converts mucus, forces lungs and spleen, dries out, passes
downwardly.
Cooking time approx. 10 min
Calories p. portion: 0
4 portions

Quantity of ingredients
Thyme 3 table spoons / 6g. (rec.) - warm - bitter.. *
Water 2 cup water / 500g. (yes) - cool - salty ....earth

Cooking instructions:
Heat the water till it boils and put it aside. Add thyme and 10 min. to let
go. Strain. Sweet to taste with honey.
Drink 2 to 3 cups daily by mouth

9.24 Tea Green tea

Reduces internal heat, dissolves mucus, detoxifies.
Cooking time approx. 10 min
Calories p. portion: 2
1 portions

Quantity of ingredients
Green tea 1 teaspoon / 2g. (rec.) - cool - sweet, bitter ....fire
Water 1 cup / 120g. (yes) - cool - salty..earth

Cooking instructions:
For each cup you use a teaspoonful or a teabag.
Pour green tea only with 60 to 80 ° C / 140 to 176 °F hot water,
otherwise it will be bitter.
If the tea has a stimulating effect, let it draw for two to three minutes. It
has a calming effect for a duration of five minutes (no longer, otherwise
it will be bitter!).
Another method: Pour the tea leaves with about 70 ° C / 158 °F hot
water and pour the water immediately again. Then just pour hot water
again. The bitter substances disappear and the tea gets a milder
aroma.

9.25 Thick pea soup

Nourishes Qi, diuretic, harmonizes Qi (especially in the Middle and Lower), strengthens the kidney and the defense Qi, dischars moisture.
Cooking time approx. 2-3 hours
Calories p. portion: 123
3 portions
Allergens: AN

Quantity of ingredients

Peas, green 3/8 lbs - 6oz / 150g. (yes) - neutral - sweet............................ water
Water 2 1/4 cups / 550g. (yes) - cool - salty ....earth
Sesame oil 1 table spoon / 20g. (little) - cool - sweet ....earth
Onion white 1/2 piece / 25g. (yes) - warm - acrid .... metal
Ginger fresh 1/2 teaspoon / 1g. (rec.) - warm - acrid................................ metal
Ground 1/2 teaspoon / 1g. (rec.) - warm - acrid .... metal
Oat meal 1 table spoon / 15g. (yes) - warm - sweet................................... metal
Salt 1 pinch / 1g. (yes) - cold - salty .... water
Parsley 1 stem / 2g. (rec.) - warm - bitter .... wood

Cooking instructions:
Soak dried peas before cooking. Sauté sesame oil, onion, a little oatmeal, ginger and cumin in a hot pot; add the peas and simmer for 2-3 hours; add salt at the end and prué with a blender; garnish with parsley.

9.26 Tsampa

Reduces internal heat, dissolves mucus, detoxifies.
Cooking time approx. 5 min
Calories p. portion: 140
2 portions
Allergens: A

Quantity of ingredients

Tsampa (roasted barley flour) 4 table spoons / 30g. () - cold - sweet, little salty
    earth
Green tea 1 cup / 120g. (rec.) - cool - sweet, bitter ....fire
Water 1 cup / 120g. (yes) - cool - salty..earth

Cooking instructions:

Tsampa is traditionally made with tea.
The tsampa is poured into a bowl and doused with tea, part of which is drunk and the remainder made into a dough-like mass with tsampa.
You can also pour the tea first; In any case, it takes some skill to

achieve the right balance of tsampa and liquid. The two substances are usually mixed with your fingers. It is recommended to add yak butter to improve taste and stability.

9.27 Vegetable miso soup with tofu

Strengthens spleen and liver, regulates Qi flow, moisturizes, relaxes, builds up Qi, spreads, forces Qi, forces liver and kidney, reduces damp heat, detoxifies, nourishes fluids, reduces internal heat, dries out, passes downwardly.
Cooking time approx. 15 min
Calories p. portion: 107
4 portions
Allergens: EN

Quantity of ingredients
Sesame oil 2 table spoons / 35g. (little) - cool - sweet ....earth
Onion (shallot) 1 piece / 20g. (yes) - warm - acrid, sweet ....metal
Carrot 1 piece / 70g. (rec.) - neutral - sweet...earth
Leek 2 inches / 10g. (yes) - warm - acrid ....metal
Water 3 cups / 750g. (yes) - cool - salty ....earth
Endive salad 2 table spoons / 30g. (rec.) - neutral - bitter............................fire
Soy Tofu 2 table spoons / 30g. (yes) - cool - sweet ....earth
Ginger fresh 1/2 teaspoon / 1g. (rec.) - warm - acrid...................................metal
Miso 2 table spoons / 15g. (rec.) - neutral - salty ....water

Cooking instructions:
In sesame oil first sauté onions, then carrots and a little leek; Pour in water and simmer gently; add the bean sprouts and endive leaves and leave to stand; Tofu cubes, add a little ginger; at the end stir in a little cooled cooking-water the Miso.

10 Effects of food

10.1 Use ingredients: recommendable

Apple (sweet)
Bamboo shoots
Barley
Barley malt
Basil
Basil (fresh)
Batavia
Bitter orange peel
Black caraway

Carrot
Carrot (Early Carrot)
Carrot juice without sugar
Celery sticks
Chervil
Chicory
Corn Grease (Polenta)
Dill
Endive salad

Ginger fresh
Grapefruit (Pomelo)
Grapefruit juice
Green tea
Ground
Ground caraway
Hawthorn
Kiwi
Lamb's lettuce
Leaf salads (bitter)
Lettuce
Mango
Miso
Mung bean sprouting

Oregano dried
Parsley
Pepper white (ground)
Pineapple
Pineapple (from a can)
Pineapple juice without sugar
Radicchio
Radish (white, green, purple-red)
Radish black
Romaine lettuce / lettuce salad
Savory
Spelled semolina
Thyme

10.2 Use ingredients: yes

Adzuki beans
Almond marzipan
Almond milk
Almond puree
Anchovy / Sardine
Anise (Common Fennel)
Apricot
Apricots
Barley not peeled
Basic recipe for a chicken soup
(warming)
Basic recipe for a duck soup
Basic recipe for a rice soup (Congee)
Bean oil
Bitter melon
Black tea
Black-eyed peas
Boletus mushroom
Boxhorn clover seeds
Brussels sprouts
Butter organic
Carp
Celery root
Cereal coffee
Chanterelle
Chenpi (chinese tangerine bowl)
Cherry
Chestnuts
Chinese cabbage
Chives
Clove
Coconut flakes
Coconut grated
Coconut milk
Cod
Coriander
Corn

Crucian
Cumin (Caraway seed)
Curcuma
Dates dried
Fennel
Fennel tea
Feta cheese
Fig
Fig dried
Fish pieces mixed (fresh water)
French beans
Goose egg
Gourd
Grape juice red
Grape juice white
Grapefruit dried peel
Grapes white
Grass carp
Hazelnuts
Herbs various
Herring
Hyssop
Iceberg lettuce
Juniper berry
Kohlrabi
Kumquats
Lamb shoulder
Leek
Lentils
Lentils black
Lentils red
Lentils yellow
Longane
Lovage
Lychee
Lychee in Preserved
Malt

Marjoram
Morel (black, dried)
Morel, dried
Mustard seeds
Oat flour
Oat meal
Oat milk
Octopus
Okra
Olives
Onion (shallot)
Onion (spring onion)
Onion read
Onion white
Oyster mushroom
Papaya
Parsnip
Peanut oil
Peanuts
Pearl barley
Peas
Peas, green
Peppers
Peppers (rose peppers)
Perch
Pine nuts
Pistachios
Plaice
Poppy
Potato
Pumpkin
Pumpkin seed oil
Pumpkin seeds
Quail egg
Quinoa
Raisins
Rapeseed oil
Red cabbage
Rice (whole grain)
Rice black
Rice flour
Rice long grain rice
Rice malt

Rice noodles
Rice red
Rice round grain
Rice sweet
Rice variety any
Rice wild (nature rice)
Rosemary
Rye
Rye flour
Saffron
Sago (cereals)
Salmon
Salt
Shark
Shiitake, dried
Shrimp
Sour milk cheese 20%
Soy Tofu
Soybean oil
Soybeans, black
Soybeans, yellow
Spinach
Spiny lobsters
Star anise
Sugar brown
Sugar candy white
Sunflower seeds
Sweet potato
Trout
Tuna
Turmeric (yellow root)
Turnips
Umeboshi plums (Japanese apricots)
Vanilla
Vanilla powder
Walnuts
Water
Water hot
White bread (wheat bread)
White wine
Wild boar meat
Zucchini

10.3 Use ingredients: little

Apple (sour)
Apple juice (natural cloudy)
Arrowroot
Artichoke
Balm
Beef fillet
Beef meat
Beef meat (calf)

Beef meatbones
Beer (Pils)
Beer (Top-fermented German dark beer)
Blackberry´s
Blueberry
Blueberry juice
Breadcrumbs (wheat bread, bread roll)

Broccoli
Buttermilk
Calamari
Cashews
Cauliflower
Champignon
Chicken egg
Chicken meat
Chicken yolk
Chickpeas
Chlorella (fresh water)
Coix (seeds) YiYi Ren
Couscous
Cranberry
Cranberry juice
Cream, sweet 30%
Curd cheese 20%
Curd cheese 40%
Currant (black)
Currant (red)
Currant (white)
Deer meat
Duck (heart)
Duck (slaughtered)
Elderberry blossom tee
Fresh cheese
Goat
Goat and sheep's milk
Goat cheese
Goose
Goose parts
Gooseberry
Grapes red
Kefir
Kombu seaweed (Saccharina japonica)
Lamb meat
Lemon peel
Lobster
Maple syrup
Margarine
Margarine (diet)
Millet
Millet flakes
Multi-grain bread (gray bread)

Mung bean
Mutton
Olive oil
Oysters
Pear
Pear juice
Pheasant
Pigeon
Pomegranate
Pork meat
Quail
Quince
Rabbit
Rabbit meat
Radish
Raspberry
Raspberry dried (immature)
Red wine
Reishi mushroom
Sage
Sake
Salsify
Sauerkraut (cutted cabbage fermented)
Sesame oil
Sour cherries
Sour cream 15% fat
Sour milk
Soybean milk
Strawberries
Strawberry Juice
Sunflower oil
Tangerine
Tarragon (Estragon)
Turkey breast meat
Vegetable juice
Wakame
Wheat
Wheat bulgur
Wheat flakes
Wheat flour
Wheat germ oil
Wheat semolina
Wheat semolina for children

10.4 Do not use contra-acting foods

Agar agar (kelp)
Amaranth
Asparagus (green or white)
Aubergine
Avocado
Banana
Banana (cooking banana)

Burdock root tea
Cantaloupe
Carambola (Star fruit)
Caviar
Chard
Chili (pod or ground)
Cinnamon ground

Cinnamon sticks
Cocoa
Coffee
Cow's milk (1.5% fat)
Cow's milk (whole milk 3.5% fat)
Crab
Cress
Cucumber
Curry
Dandelion (young plants)
Dandelionroots tea
Deer meat
Garlic
Ginger powder
Green spelt
Honey
Lamb's lettuce
Lemon
Lemon juice
Lime
Mallow (Malva sylvestris) blossom tea
Miso paste (soy bean paste)
Mold cheese
Mozzarella
Mulberry fruit
Mullet
Mussels
Mutton
Nutmeg
Orange
Orange juice
Parmesan
Pepper Cayenne
Peppercorns
Pickle
Pimento
Plum
Rhubarb
Rose hip
Rose hip tea
Seacrab
Sorrel
Soy sauce
Sugar white
Tomato
Vinegar (Apple vinegar)
Vinegar (Red wine vinegar)
Vinegar Aceto Balsamico
Watermelon
Wheat beer
Wheat bran
Yogi tea
Yogurt (natural, 1.5% fat)
Yogurt (natural, 3.5% fat)

11 Complementary

11.1 Cardamom

Elettaria cardamomum
Preparation: Decoction
Warms the middle, releases stagnation, leads upwards. Tonifies kidney yang, warms kidneys and spleen; strengthens stomach, astringent.
Decoction from 3-10 g, drink in two doses on an empty stomach
Do not use on: stomach ulcers
Active ingredients: fatty oil, sugar, protein, gum, starch, many other ingredients.

12 Basics of Nutrition

The basic principles of nutrition described herein are general recommendations. They are not aimed at a specific form of therapy. Recommendations concerning a therapy have priority.

12.1 Nutrition

Regular meals in a relaxed atmosphere. A warm breakfast is considered a good start into the day.
The main meals ought to be taken for lunch – supper in the early evening. Pay attention to feeling hungry or sated: don't eat too much nor remain hungry is the rule
Prepare the meals freshly from natural, regional products. Frozen, heat-conserved, industrially prepared or foodstuffs cooked in the microwave oven are rejected.
Choice of foodstuffs according to the season: more cooling food in summer, more warming food in winter.
Eat cooked food at least twice a day. Food and drinks ought to be lukewarm, never ice-cold or hot.
Raw vegetables, briefly cooked vegetables, freshly squeezed juices and mineral water are not recommended. Milk and dairy products are only included in the diet if they don't cause problems. Don't use therapeutic recipes over a longer period without consulting your doctor or therapist.

Varied food
Enjoy the diversity of foodstuffs. Characteristics of a balanced nutrition are variety, suitable combination and a balanced quantity of rich and low energy foodstuffs (on one hand avoiding undersupply with essential nutrients and on the other hand to take to many undesirable substances).

A lot of Cereal Products - and Potatoes
Bread, pasta, rice, cereal flakes (best wholemeal) as well as potatoes contain almost no fat, but many vitamins, mineral nutrients, trace elements, roughage and secondary plant substances. These foodstuffs ought to be taken with low-fat side dishes.

Vegetables and Fruit – „Take Five" every day ... 5 portions of vegetables and fruit a day, as fresh as possible, briefly cooked, or maybe one portion as a juice – ideal as a side dish to every meal as well as snack between meals: Thus a lot of vitamins, mineral nutrients as well as roughage and secondary plant substances

Daily milk and dairy products
Milk and Dairy Products every Day, once or twice per Week Fish; meat, sausages as well as eggs moderately. These foodstuffs contain valuable nutrients like calcium in the milk, iodine selenium and omega-3 fat acids in saltwater fish. Meat is favorable due to its high content of disposable iron and the vitamins B1, B6 and B12. Quantities of 300 – 600 g meat and sausage per week are sufficient. Prefer low-fat products, especially in meat- and dairy products.

Low-fat and fatty Foodstuffs
Fat supplies us with essential fat acids and fatty foodstuffs contain also fat-soluble vitamins. Fat is high in energy; therefore much fat in the food may cause overweight, possibly also cancer. Too many saturated fat acids may further a tendency for cardio-vascular diseases in the long term. Prefer vegetable oils and fats (e.g. rapeseed-, olive-, soya-oils and solid fats produced therefrom). Beware of invisible fat in meat- and dairy products, pastry and sweets as well as in fast-food and convenience foods. 70 – 90 g fat per day is sufficient.

Moderately Sugar and Salt
Take sugar and foods/drinks containing various kinds of sugar (e.g. glucose syrup) only occasionally. Use herbs and spices as well as a little salt creatively. Prefer salt containing iodine.

Plenty of Liquids
Water is absolutely essential. Drink 1-2 l liquids every day. Prefer water (with or without gas) and other low-calorie drinks. Alcoholic drinks should not be taken.

Tasty Dishes, carefully cooked
Cook the meals with as low temperatures and as short as possible, using little water and fat – this preserves the original taste, keeps the nutrients intact and prevents the production of harmful compounds.

Take time and enjoy the food
Take your Time and enjoy your Food
Eating consciously helps to eat right. The eye enjoys food, too. It's fun, invites to enjoy varied dishes and stimulates the feeling of satiety.

Watch your Weight and stay in Motion
A balanced diet and a lot of exercise and sport (30 – 60 min/day) are a healthy combination. The right weight furthers well-being and health.
Thermals, directional effectiveness, digestive power
There are various criteria for judging the effectiveness of herbs and foodstuffs.
The use of certain herbs and ingredients is based on observations of the effects on the body which these foodstuffs, herbs and spices show after having eaten them. The medical science has developed following system: Every ingredient or herb has a directional effectiveness. Furthermore, there are herbs which have a special effect on certain organs.
The basic condition for a healthy metabolism is to obtain sufficient energy from food and that the digestive process doesn't use too much energy. An easily digestible meal makes content and sated, doesn't cause flatulence and fatigue after the meal. The perfect spices increase the healthiness of our meals. Very often, just small doses of herbs and spices will suffice. They are not used to make us sated, but to help our digestive organs to digest the food.

12.2 Recipes

The recipes list the ingredients to be used and the cooking instructions show how the dish is prepared. The list of ingredients shows the concerned quantities as well as the relevance for the therapy. If you find „less than mentioned", try to comply or find an alternative from the „list of recommended foodstuffs". Mostly it shall result just in a small change

of taste when you simply avoid this ingredient.
Mild cooking methods: boiling, stewing, poaching, steaming
Strong cooking methods: barbecuing, roasting, frying, smoking
Balanced cooking methods: deep-frying, baking brick
Deep-freezing and warming in the microwave oven should be avoided
(denaturalization).

12.3 Foodstuffs

Foodstuffs have an effect on body and soul like medicinal herbs, only a
very much milder one. Dietary advice is mainly based on regional
foodstuffs. The knowledge about the effects of each foodstuff and the
knowledge, when which foodstuff shall be used, is based on the
orthodoschool of medicine. Use ecologic-organic products, if possible.
As everything should be cooked for a long time due to a better
digestability and very rarely eaten raw, the food agrees with everyone.
The classification of the foodstuffs according to their effect on the body
is the basis in order to achieve a harmonious status of health.
Dietary advisors do not recommend certain foodstuffs for everyone. The
individual diet is tailor-made for the individual constitution.

Buy only fresh and ripe fruit and vegetables. You ought to leave unripe
fruit and vegetables and such with brown spots and wilted leaves
behind in the market. In this case take deep-frozen goods (never ready-
to-serve dishes!). Fruit and vegetables are deep-frozen immediately
after harvesting and often contain more vitamins and minerals than the
goods from the vegetable shelf. Whereas conserved or tinned goods
contain very much less biological substances. Also, salt, sugar and
others are mostly added to the latter. Never leave the foodstuffs in the
water after washing them to avoid that many vital substances get
drowned. Clean salads, fruit and vegetables immediately before
serving.

Please make sure of the hygienic processing of foodstuffs. Clean your
salads, fruit and vegetables carefully. When cooking with meat, prepare
all ingredients first and then process the meat products. Clean the
worktop and tools very carefully. Wooden surfaces ought to be treated
with a mild disinfectant regularly in order to reduce germination.
Store fruit and vegetables separately, if possible. Harvested fruit and
vegetables are still alive and emit e.g. ethylene gas, which makes other
products ripen and age faster. Keep meat and fish in the closed
packaging or store them in the fridge in closed containers.

12.4 Herbs

There are some basic rules for storing medicinal herbs. On principle, herbs must be protected from direct sunlight, humidity and heat.

Containers for the storage of herbs may be glasses, ceramic jars and even plastic containers. However, plastic is a rather unsuitable material and should only be a short-term solution. In case of glass containers, use a dark material.

Medicinal herbs cannot be kept for any long period. The shelf life of herbs is limited. However, it can be prolonged with suitable storage. The place should be dark, rather cool and absolutely dry. A wooden medicine cabinet, placed not directly next to a source of heat, would be ideal. Never buy large quantities of herbs so as not to have to throw them away. Label the container with the name of the herb and the date of harvesting or processing.

13 Other dietic-books

The following syndromes of dietetics, TCM or for a therapy supplement for cancer are available.

Dietetics

E001. Nutrition of the infant - baby food
E002. Nutrition during lactation
E003. Nutrition in old age
E004. Nutrition of children and adolescents
E005. Nutrition of athletes
E006. Light weight
E007. Pregnancy
E008. Full food

Protein and electrolyte - kidneys
E009. (hemodialysis) dialysis treatment
E010. Acute renal failure
E011. Chronic renal insufficiency
E012. Nephrotic syndrome
E013. Kidney stones (nephrolithiasis)

Gastrointestinal tract - pancreas
E014. Acute pancreatitis (inflammation of the pancreas)
E015. Chronic pancreatitis (inflammation of the pancreas)

Gastrointestinal tract - small intestine and large intestine
E016. Acute obstipation (constipation)
E017. Chronic obstipation (constipation)
E018. Colon irritabile
E019. Diverticulitis
E020. Acquired lactose intolerance (lactose malabsorption)
E021. Fructose malabsorption
E022. Glutensensitive enteropathy (celiac disease)
E023. Colectomy
E024. Short Bowel Syndrome

Gastrointestinal tract - liver, gallbladder, bile ducts
E025. Acute and chronic hepatitis (inflammation of the liver)
E026. Cholelithiasis (bile stones)
E027. fatty liver
E028. cirrhosis

Gastrointestinal tract - Stomach and duodenal intestine
E029. Acute gastritis
E030. Chronic gastritis
E031. Stomach bleeding
E032. Ulcus ventriculi and duodenal ulcer
E033. Condition after gastric surgery

Gastrointestinal tract - oral cavity and esophagus
E034. Stomatitis
E035. Esophageal carcinoma (esophageal cancer)
E036. Refluosophagitis (heartburn)

Special diseases
E037. Phenylketonuria (PKU)
E038. Rheumatic joint diseases

Metabolism
E039. Obesity (overweight)
E040. Diabetes mellitus
E041. Eating disorders (underweight)

Fat metabolism
E042. Hypercholesterolaemia (increased cholesterol level)
E043. Hepatic Encephalopathy

Heart and circulation
E044. Arteriosclerosis (arterial calcification)
E045. Heart insufficiency
E046. Hypertension
E047. Hyperuricaemia and gout

Changed nutrient requirements
E048. In case of fever
E049. For malignant diseases
E050. After burns
E051. Radiation and chemotherapy

CANCER
E100. Pancreatic cancer
E101. Bladder cancer
E102. Blood cancer (leukemia)
E103. Breast cancer
E104. Colorectal cancer
E105. Gastric cancer
E106. Kidney cancer
E107. Esophageal cancer

TCM
E200. Bladder - moisture heat in the bladder
E201. Bladder - moisture and cold in the bladder
E202. Bladder - emptiness and cold in the bladder
E203. Large intestine - external cold affects the large intestine
E204. Large intestine - moisture heat in the large intestine
E205. Large intestine - heat blocks the intestine II acute
E206. Large intestine - dryness of the colon
E207. Large intestine - Yang deficiency (cold)
E208. Heart - Blood insufficiency
E209. Heart - Blood stagnation

E210. Heart - Fire
E211. Heart - Hot mucus clogs the heart pores
E212. Heart - Cold mucus clogs the heart pores
E213. Heart - Qi deficiency
E214. Heart - Yang deficiency
E215. Heart - Yin deficiency
E216. Liver - Ascending Liver Yang
E217. Liver - Blood deficiency
E218. Liver - Blood stagnation
E219. Liver - Moisture heat in liver and gall bladder
E220. Liver - Fire
E221. Liver - Gall bladder Qi-Empty
E222. Liver - Cold in the liver meridian
E223. Liver - Qi stagnation
E224. Liver - Wind
E225. Liver - Wind with ascending liver Yang
E226. Liver - Wind with blood anemic
E227. Liver - Wind with extreme heat
E228. Lung - Qi deficiency
E229. Lung - Mucus-moisture in the lungs
E230. Lung - Mucus-heat in the lungs
E231. Lung - Mucus-cold in the lungs
E232. Lung - Dryness of the lungs
E233. Lung - Wind-heat attacks the lungs
E234. Lung - Wind-cold affects the lungs
E235. Lung - Yin deficiency
E236. Stomach - Bloodstagnation
E237. Stomach - Fire
E238. Stomach - Cold with liquid
E239. Stomach - Nutrition stagnation
E240. Stomach - Qi deficiency
E241. Stomach - Rebellious Qi
E242. Stomach - Yin Emptiness
E243. Spleen - Heat and moisture attack the spleen
E244. Spleen - Coldness and moisture affects the spleen
E245. Spleen - Qi deficiency
E246. Spleen - Qi deficiency + Declining spleen Qi
E247. Spleen - Qi deficiency + spleen does not control the blood
E248. Spleen - Yang deficiency
E249. Kidney - Heart and kidney no longer communicate
E250. Kidney - Jing deficiency
E251. Kidney - Kidneys cannot receive the Qi
E252. Kidney - Qi is not stable
E253. Kidney - Yang deficiency
E254. Kidney - Yin deficiency

For further information visit nutribook.info.

14 EBNS - Software for nutritional counseling

The main task of the database is to create personalized nutritional advice for each patient individually. The database was developed for

Dietetics and Traditional Chinese Medicine.
The Database supports training and advices in the daily work routine.

The computer program provides lists of recipes, ingredients and herbs, which are given to the client. individually adjustable according to patient's request from whole food to vegetarians (lacto, ovo, ...). For every register there is an information sheet which can be given to the client. All texts can be individually designed.

The syndromes can be combined and result in an intersection of the recommended recipes and ingredients. The automated diagnosis for the TCM enables you to check your experience during the training as well as to confirm your diagnosis in the working day. You select several predefined symptoms and have the program automatically display the relevant syndromes.

How to work with the database:
Select the patient / client, select one or more of the syndromes you diagnosed and print the folder.

You can change all values, create new symptoms or syndromes, develop recipes, change or adapt ingredients and herbs to your findings. In simple client management, all relevant data about the person is stored. You get an overview of the past diagnoses and the development of the course of the disease.

As a consultant you save a lot of time when you print out the recipe, food and herbal lists for the recognized syndromes and give them to the clients. You can use this time for a personal conversation. With the database, dieticians and nutritionists can view the nutrients and trace elements for each recipe and develop recipes for syndromes even with suggested ingredients.

All recipe and grocery lists can also be ordered from me as a combination of several diseases. I wish all readers good luck, health and happiness in life.
More information can be found at www.ebns.at.
Volunteer: www.krebsinfo.at
Josef Miligui